Higher Scores on Social Studie[s]
Grade 3

MW01251294

Table of Contents

Introduction

This book is a tool to help your students prepare for taking standardized tests. Research shows that students who are acquainted with the scoring format of standardized tests score higher on those tests. Students also score higher when they understand the pressures of time limits and have practice taking timed tests. The concepts presented in this book are found on typical standardized tests for this grade level. Practice activities include reading comprehension, analyzing tables and graphs, and using maps. The scores on these activities are an indication of a student's ability to take tests, not necessarily to master the concepts or content used for practice.

The book is divided into four units, each focusing on a particular area of social studies skill: History, Geography, Government, and Economics. The book's structure has two parts. In the first part are the unit pretests and a general posttest. These tests can be used as diagnostic tools. The pretests will help students become familiar with the content of each unit as well as prepare students for the formats of multiple choice and short answer. The posttest can serve as a practice test and encompasses multiple choice, short answer, and extended response formats.

The second part of the book focuses on specific skills particular to the four units of study in social studies. It provides students with practice in typical test-taking formats that they can expect to see. Each unit has three parts. Part 1 provides practice in answering multiple choice questions. Students darken circles on a separate, reproducible answer sheet provided on page 2 of this book. Part 2 develops skills in writing short answers based on an informational paragraph or a graphic organizer. Students write answers on the Part 2 pages. In Part 3, students draw on background knowledge to write a long, organized response on pages provided in the tests. From time to time, students are encouraged to evaluate their performance. Again, the goal of the book is to improve the students' ability to perform well on standardized tests.

Note

On page 3 is a letter to students explaining useful tips for each testing format. Before beginning the testing practice, give each student the letter and review the information.

Higher Scores on Social Studies Standardized Tests
Grade 3 Answer Sheet

STUDENT'S NAME:

LAST   FIRST   MI

SCHOOL:

TEACHER:

FEMALE ○   MALE ○

BIRTH DATE

MONTH	DAY	YEAR
Jan ○	⓪ ⓪	⓪ ⓪
Feb ○	① ①	① ①
Mar ○	② ②	② ②
Apr ○	③ ③	③ ③
May ○	④	④ ④
Jun ○	⑤	⑤ ⑤
Jul ○	⑥	⑥ ⑥
Aug ○	⑦	⑦ ⑦
Sep ○	⑧	⑧ ⑧
Oct ○	⑨	⑨ ⑨
Nov ○		
Dec ○		

GRADE   ② ③ ④ ⑤ ⑥

Higher Scores on Social Studies Standardized Tests, Grade 3
© Steck-Vaughn Company

(Name grid columns: letters A through Z bubbles)

History Pretest Part 1

1. Ⓐ Ⓑ Ⓒ Ⓓ   2. Ⓐ Ⓑ Ⓒ Ⓓ   3. Ⓐ Ⓑ Ⓒ Ⓓ   4. Ⓐ Ⓑ Ⓒ Ⓓ   5. Ⓐ Ⓑ Ⓒ Ⓓ   6. Ⓐ Ⓑ Ⓒ Ⓓ

Geography Pretest Part 1

1. Ⓐ Ⓑ Ⓒ Ⓓ   2. Ⓐ Ⓑ Ⓒ Ⓓ   3. Ⓐ Ⓑ Ⓒ Ⓓ   4. Ⓐ Ⓑ Ⓒ Ⓓ   5. Ⓐ Ⓑ Ⓒ Ⓓ   6. Ⓐ Ⓑ Ⓒ Ⓓ

Government Pretest Part 1

1. Ⓐ Ⓑ Ⓒ Ⓓ   2. Ⓐ Ⓑ Ⓒ Ⓓ   3. Ⓐ Ⓑ Ⓒ Ⓓ   4. Ⓐ Ⓑ Ⓒ Ⓓ   5. Ⓐ Ⓑ Ⓒ Ⓓ   6. Ⓐ Ⓑ Ⓒ Ⓓ

Economics Pretest Part 1

1. Ⓐ Ⓑ Ⓒ Ⓓ   2. Ⓐ Ⓑ Ⓒ Ⓓ   3. Ⓐ Ⓑ Ⓒ Ⓓ   4. Ⓐ Ⓑ Ⓒ Ⓓ   5. Ⓐ Ⓑ Ⓒ Ⓓ   6. Ⓐ Ⓑ Ⓒ Ⓓ

General Posttest Part 1

1. Ⓐ Ⓑ Ⓒ Ⓓ   2. Ⓐ Ⓑ Ⓒ Ⓓ   3. Ⓐ Ⓑ Ⓒ Ⓓ   4. Ⓐ Ⓑ Ⓒ Ⓓ   5. Ⓐ Ⓑ Ⓒ Ⓓ   6. Ⓐ Ⓑ Ⓒ Ⓓ
7. Ⓐ Ⓑ Ⓒ Ⓓ   8. Ⓐ Ⓑ Ⓒ Ⓓ   9. Ⓐ Ⓑ Ⓒ Ⓓ   10. Ⓐ Ⓑ Ⓒ Ⓓ

Unit 1: History Part 1

1. Ⓐ Ⓑ Ⓒ Ⓓ   2. Ⓐ Ⓑ Ⓒ Ⓓ   3. Ⓐ Ⓑ Ⓒ Ⓓ   4. Ⓐ Ⓑ Ⓒ Ⓓ   5. Ⓐ Ⓑ Ⓒ Ⓓ   6. Ⓐ Ⓑ Ⓒ Ⓓ
7. Ⓐ Ⓑ Ⓒ Ⓓ   8. Ⓐ Ⓑ Ⓒ Ⓓ   9. Ⓐ Ⓑ Ⓒ Ⓓ   10. Ⓐ Ⓑ Ⓒ Ⓓ   11. Ⓐ Ⓑ Ⓒ Ⓓ   12. Ⓐ Ⓑ Ⓒ Ⓓ
13. Ⓐ Ⓑ Ⓒ Ⓓ   14. Ⓐ Ⓑ Ⓒ Ⓓ

Unit 2: Geography Part 1

1. Ⓐ Ⓑ Ⓒ Ⓓ   2. Ⓐ Ⓑ Ⓒ Ⓓ   3. Ⓐ Ⓑ Ⓒ Ⓓ   4. Ⓐ Ⓑ Ⓒ Ⓓ   5. Ⓐ Ⓑ Ⓒ Ⓓ   6. Ⓐ Ⓑ Ⓒ Ⓓ
7. Ⓐ Ⓑ Ⓒ Ⓓ   8. Ⓐ Ⓑ Ⓒ Ⓓ   9. Ⓐ Ⓑ Ⓒ Ⓓ   10. Ⓐ Ⓑ Ⓒ Ⓓ   11. Ⓐ Ⓑ Ⓒ Ⓓ   12. Ⓐ Ⓑ Ⓒ Ⓓ
13. Ⓐ Ⓑ Ⓒ Ⓓ   14. Ⓐ Ⓑ Ⓒ Ⓓ

Unit 3: Government Part 1

1. Ⓐ Ⓑ Ⓒ Ⓓ   2. Ⓐ Ⓑ Ⓒ Ⓓ   3. Ⓐ Ⓑ Ⓒ Ⓓ   4. Ⓐ Ⓑ Ⓒ Ⓓ   5. Ⓐ Ⓑ Ⓒ Ⓓ   6. Ⓐ Ⓑ Ⓒ Ⓓ
7. Ⓐ Ⓑ Ⓒ Ⓓ   8. Ⓐ Ⓑ Ⓒ Ⓓ   9. Ⓐ Ⓑ Ⓒ Ⓓ   10. Ⓐ Ⓑ Ⓒ Ⓓ   11. Ⓐ Ⓑ Ⓒ Ⓓ   12. Ⓐ Ⓑ Ⓒ Ⓓ
13. Ⓐ Ⓑ Ⓒ Ⓓ   14. Ⓐ Ⓑ Ⓒ Ⓓ

Unit 4: Economics Part 1

1. Ⓐ Ⓑ Ⓒ Ⓓ   2. Ⓐ Ⓑ Ⓒ Ⓓ   3. Ⓐ Ⓑ Ⓒ Ⓓ   4. Ⓐ Ⓑ Ⓒ Ⓓ   5. Ⓐ Ⓑ Ⓒ Ⓓ   6. Ⓐ Ⓑ Ⓒ Ⓓ
7. Ⓐ Ⓑ Ⓒ Ⓓ   8. Ⓐ Ⓑ Ⓒ Ⓓ   9. Ⓐ Ⓑ Ⓒ Ⓓ   10. Ⓐ Ⓑ Ⓒ Ⓓ

Dear Student,

Sometime this year, this class will take a special test. This test might include multiple choice questions, short answer questions, and a writing exercise. The writing exercise will require a long, written response based on general information you have learned in school.

To help you prepare for this test, we will soon begin to take practice tests. The practice tests will help you become familiar with the different kinds of questions you will see. Below you will find some tips to help you use your testing time wisely and to help you focus on the important skills.

For Multiple Choice Questions:
- Read each question carefully.
- Then, read all of the answer choices.
- Check to make sure the item number and the number on the answer sheet match.
- Darken the circle completely.
- If you make a mistake, carefully erase the pencil mark.
- Review each question and answer if you have time.

For Short Answer Questions:
- Read the directions carefully. Some directions ask that you answer in complete sentences.
- Quickly review the questions before reading the paragraph or studying the graphic.
- Then, read the paragraph or study the graphic.
- Check your answers by looking back at the paragraph or graphic.
- Review your answers to check for correct grammar and punctuation.

For Extended Response Questions:
- Read the directions carefully.
- Review the question before reading the paragraph or studying the graphic. Be sure you know what the task is.
- Then, read the information given.
- Make a brief outline that shows the main idea and supporting details you wish to include in your response.
- Remember to write a short introduction stating what you plan to cover and a conclusion summing up your answer.
- Reread the question to make sure you covered all the points.
- Review your paragraphs to check for correct grammar and punctuation.

Remember, these tests are only a practice. Good luck!

History Pretest

Your score: _____

Part 1: Multiple Choice

Directions Darken the circle by the correct answer.

⏱ **You have 15 minutes to complete the History test.**

1. What does the Constitution describe?
- Ⓐ how states can build roads
- Ⓑ how the United States government works
- Ⓒ how the city government must give service
- Ⓓ how people need to show their patriotism

2. Who wrote "The Star Spangled Banner"?
- Ⓐ George Washington
- Ⓑ Ben Franklin
- Ⓒ Francis Scott Key
- Ⓓ Martin Luther King

3. What is the love of one's country?
- Ⓐ patriotism
- Ⓑ liberty
- Ⓒ freedom
- Ⓓ public

4. What kind of shelter is made from the skin of animals?
- Ⓐ cabin
- Ⓑ tepee
- Ⓒ hut
- Ⓓ canoe

5. What is the name of a person who explores and settles in a new area first?
- Ⓐ pioneer
- Ⓑ worker
- Ⓒ mayor
- Ⓓ slave

6. Which of these symbols in New York harbor stands for freedom and hope?

Ⓐ   Ⓑ

Ⓒ  Ⓓ

GO ON ⇨

History Pretest, page 2

Part 2: Short Answer

Directions Use the time line to answer exercises 7 through 10.

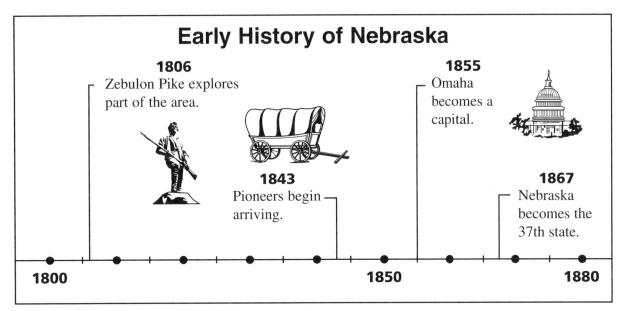

Early History of Nebraska

1806
Zebulon Pike explores part of the area.

1843
Pioneers begin arriving.

1855
Omaha becomes a capital.

1867
Nebraska becomes the 37th state.

1800   1850   1880

7. What years does this time line cover?

_____

8. What year did Zebulon Pike explore the area?

_____

9. What happened first—Nebraska became a state or Omaha was made the capital?

_____

10. How many years passed between when the pioneers came to the state and when Nebraska became a state?

_____

Geography Pretest

Your score: _____

Part 1: Multiple Choice

Directions   Darken the circle by the correct answer.

⏱ **You have 15 minutes to complete the Geography test.**

1. What kind of land is surrounded on all sides by water?
   Ⓐ a plain
   Ⓑ a mountain
   Ⓒ a river
   Ⓓ an island

2. What does a compass rose show?
   Ⓐ capitals
   Ⓑ highways
   Ⓒ directions
   Ⓓ distances

3. What do people find in the ground when they dig?
   Ⓐ minerals
   Ⓑ numbers
   Ⓒ laws
   Ⓓ maps

4. Why do states have capitals?
   Ⓐ Business people always meet there.
   Ⓑ Government leaders meet there.
   Ⓒ Only librarians work there.
   Ⓓ It is where schoolteachers learn to teach.

5. What are schools and parks?
   Ⓐ public places
   Ⓑ businesses
   Ⓒ natural resources
   Ⓓ landforms

6. Which of theses names a natural resource?
   Ⓐ climate
   Ⓑ forest
   Ⓒ store
   Ⓓ farm

GO ON ⇨

Geography Pretest, page 2

Part 2: Short Answer

Directions   Read the story below. Think about information you know related to communities. Then, complete the exercise.

The town of Henryville is in the southern part of the United States. The winters are mostly warm. It never snows there. Many people have moved to Henryville because of its fine weather.

Other people have moved to Henryville because of jobs. Some people work at a college. Others work in a clothing factory there. Lately, some people have come to work in a new computer company.

Henryville is a place where people help one another meet needs. People there have worked together to build fine schools, hospitals, libraries, and parks. The people of Henryville are proud of their town.

Write a paragraph explaining why Henryville is a good community in which to live.

_____

_____

_____

_____

_____

_____

_____   **STOP**

Name _____   Date _____

Government Pretest

Your score: _____

Part 1: Multiple Choice

Directions Darken the circle by the correct answer.

⏱ **You have 15 minutes to complete the Government test.**

1. Which of these names the rules in a community?
    - Ⓐ orders
    - Ⓑ service
    - Ⓒ laws
    - Ⓓ choices

2. Who is the leader of the United States?
    - Ⓐ a king
    - Ⓑ a President
    - Ⓒ a police officer
    - Ⓓ a judge

3. Why do people pay taxes?
    - Ⓐ to pay for schools and police
    - Ⓑ to pay for stores
    - Ⓒ to pay for dentists and doctors
    - Ⓓ to pay for factories

4. What do members of Congress do?
    - Ⓐ make laws for the whole country
    - Ⓑ set up statues to honor soldiers
    - Ⓒ decide if a national law is broken
    - Ⓓ work in the White House

5. Which of these is NOT a rule for being a responsible citizen?
    - Ⓐ putting litter in a trash can
    - Ⓑ crossing streets in cross walks
    - Ⓒ writing on a store building
    - Ⓓ turning off lights

6. How is a mayor in a community chosen?
    - Ⓐ The fastest runner in a race wins.
    - Ⓑ A judge chooses the mayor.
    - Ⓒ The oldest person wins.
    - Ⓓ The people in that community vote.

GO ON ⇨

Government Pretest, page 2

Part 2: Short Answer

Directions There is talk in your town that some nearby land might be turned into a state park. Think about the information you know related to government. Then, complete the exercise.

Write a letter giving your opinion of a park. In your letter, include to whom you would address the letter, your opinion, and two reasons supporting your opinion.

Dear _____,

_____

_____

_____

_____

_____

_____

_____

_____

_____

Sincerely,

_____

Economics Pretest

Your score: _____

Part 1: Multiple Choice

Directions Darken the circle by the correct answer.

🕐 **You have 15 minutes to complete the Economics test.**

1. Which of these names things a person must have to live?
   - Ⓐ needs
   - Ⓑ service
   - Ⓒ wants
   - Ⓓ having

2. Which of these is a factory job?
   - Ⓐ selling televisions
   - Ⓑ cleaning houses
   - Ⓒ cutting hair
   - Ⓓ sewing clothes

3. What is money paid for work?
   - Ⓐ loans
   - Ⓑ savings
   - Ⓒ charges
   - Ⓓ wages

4. What is a consumer?
   - Ⓐ a person who owns a farm
   - Ⓑ a person who makes goods in a factory
   - Ⓒ a person who buys goods
   - Ⓓ a person who works in a hospital

5. What are the tools, machines, and materials that make doing things easier?
   - Ⓐ technology
   - Ⓑ school
   - Ⓒ trade
   - Ⓓ shopping

6. Which of these buys or sells things that people want?
   - Ⓐ a product
   - Ⓑ a business
   - Ⓒ a bank
   - Ⓓ a community

GO ON ⇨

Economics Pretest, page 2

Part 2: Short Answer

Directions   Study the map. Use complete sentences to answer the questions.

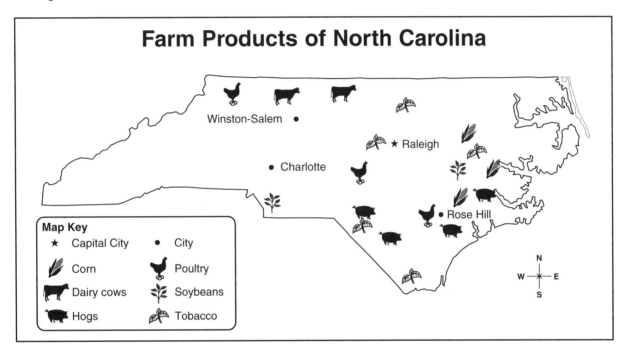

Farm Products of North Carolina

Map Key
★ Capital City   • City
🌽 Corn   🐓 Poultry
🐄 Dairy cows   🌿 Soybeans
🐖 Hogs   🍃 Tobacco

7. What is the farm product grown closest to the state capital?

_____

_____

8. Which three products are grown or raised near the town of Rose Hill?

_____

_____

9. What is the land probably like north of Rose Hill? Explain.

_____

_____

STOP

General Posttest

Your score: _____

Part 1: Multiple Choice

Directions   Darken the circle by the correct answer.

⏱ **You have 10 minutes.**

1. What are canyons and plains?
- Ⓐ weather
- Ⓑ mountains
- Ⓒ landforms
- Ⓓ minerals

2. Where are suburbs found?
- Ⓐ in the center of a city
- Ⓑ in a rural area
- Ⓒ near an ocean
- Ⓓ near a large city

3. What kinds of jobs do most workers have?
- Ⓐ factory
- Ⓑ farms
- Ⓒ service
- Ⓓ construction

4. Why do communities have rules?
- Ⓐ to help fight fires
- Ⓑ to help keep things safe and fair
- Ⓒ to help leaders run for office
- Ⓓ to help people play games

5. Which of these names what people pass down and do the same way for many years?
- Ⓐ family
- Ⓑ freedom
- Ⓒ tradition
- Ⓓ holiday

6. Why are there 50 stars on the United States flag?
- Ⓐ The stars stand for the Presidents of the United States.
- Ⓑ One star is added to the flag every ten years.
- Ⓒ The stars are for the heroes of the country.
- Ⓓ There is one star for each state.

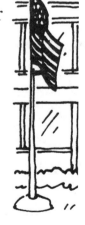

GO ON ⇨

General Posttest

Part 1, page 2

Directions Use the map to answer exercises 7 through 10.

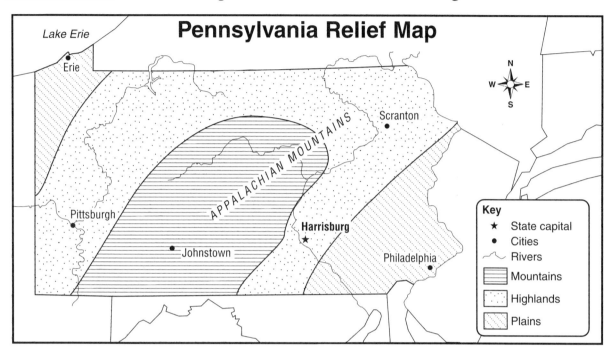

Pennsylvania Relief Map

Lake Erie
Erie
Scranton
APPALACHIAN MOUNTAINS
Pittsburgh
Harrisburg
Johnstown
Philadelphia

Key
★ State capital
• Cities
∿ Rivers
▤ Mountains
⋮ Highlands
╱ Plains

7. Which city has a port on a lake?
   Ⓐ Erie
   Ⓑ Harrisburg
   Ⓒ Philadelphia
   Ⓓ Scranton

8. Which city is most likely to have a stadium named *Three Rivers Stadium*?
   Ⓐ Harrisburg
   Ⓑ Scranton
   Ⓒ Pittsburgh
   Ⓓ Johnstown

9. What is the most common landform in Pennsylvania?
   Ⓐ swamps
   Ⓑ highlands
   Ⓒ plains
   Ⓓ mountains

10. If this map showed the highest point in Pennsylvania, near which city do you think it would be?
    Ⓐ Erie
    Ⓑ Harrisburg
    Ⓒ Johnstown
    Ⓓ Philadelphia

STOP

General Posttest

Part 2: Short Answer

Directions   Study the map. Use complete sentences to answer the questions.

⏱ **You have 15 minutes.**

Precipitation in the Southwest Region

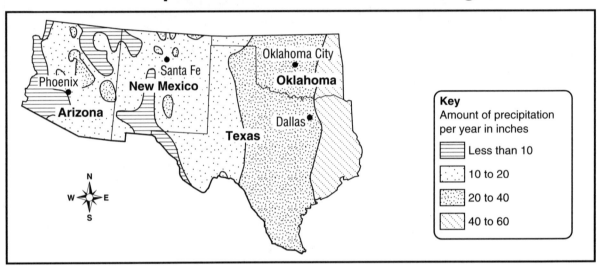

1. About how much rain does Phoenix, Arizona, receive each year?

_____

2. What part of Oklahoma receives 40 to 60 inches of rain a year?

_____

_____

3. How can you use the map to explain why cattle ranching is common in western Texas, while farming is common in eastern Texas?

_____

_____

_____   **GO ON ⇨**

General Posttest

Part 2, page 2

Directions Read the paragraph and study the drawing. Think about other information you know related to pioneers. Then, complete the exercise.

In Arizona, some Navajo families used to live in houses called **hogans**. Hogans were built of logs and then sealed with mud. The sun hardened the mud-like cement. Pioneers also used logs and mud to make houses, too. Their homes were called **log cabins**.

Suppose a pioneer sees a hogan for the first time. How might the pioneer describe the house in a letter to a friend? Complete the letter using compare and contrast.

Dear John,

_____

_____

_____

_____

_____

_____

_____

_____

Your friend,
Thomas

STOP

General Posttest

Part 3: Extended Response

Directions   Read the paragraph. Think about other information you know related to history, geography, government, and economics. Then, complete the exercise.

You have 15 minutes.

A community is a place where people live and work together. It provides for all of the people's needs. It also has activities and places that provide for their wants.

How do people decide where to build a community?

_____

_____

Be sure to...

   use complete sentences.

   give examples.

   write neatly.

_____

_____

_____

_____

_____

_____

_____

_____

GO ON ⇨

Name _____ Date _____

General Posttest

Part 3, page 2

_____

_____

_____

_____

_____

_____

_____

_____

_____

_____

_____

_____

_____

_____ **STOP**

Reread your answer to see that you...

    used complete sentences.

    gave examples.

    wrote neatly.

UNIT 1: HISTORY

Part 1: Multiple Choice

Directions Darken the circle by the correct answer.

Sample:

Who helped the Plymouth settlers?

Ⓐ Squanto
Ⓑ George Washington
Ⓒ King Henry
Ⓓ Pocahontas

Answer

The correct answer is *A. Squanto* was a friendly American Indian who showed the Pilgrims how to hunt and which seeds to plant.

Now Try These

⏱ **You have 15 minutes.**

1. Who were the first people to live in the United States?
   Ⓐ colonists
   Ⓑ immigrants
   Ⓒ American Indians
   Ⓓ Europeans

2. What is the name of a person who starts a community?
   Ⓐ mayor
   Ⓑ founder
   Ⓒ chief
   Ⓓ king

3. What is a special celebration to remember a person or event important to the people of a community?
   Ⓐ heritage
   Ⓑ religion
   Ⓒ story
   Ⓓ holiday

4. Of the following people, who found America first?
   Ⓐ Christopher Columbus
   Ⓑ John Smith
   Ⓒ Ben Franklin
   Ⓓ John Cabot

GO ON ⇨

UNIT 1: HISTORY

Part 1, page 2

5. What was the name of the war fought between America and England?
Ⓐ French Revolution
Ⓑ World War I
Ⓒ Civil War
Ⓓ The American Revolution

6. What day is the birthday for the United States?
Ⓐ July Fourth
Ⓑ May Fifth
Ⓒ December 25
Ⓓ November 24

7. Who was the first President of the United States?
Ⓐ Abraham Lincoln
Ⓑ George Bush
Ⓒ George Washington
Ⓓ Thomas Jefferson

8. What bird is a symbol of our country and its freedom?
Ⓐ turkey
Ⓑ eagle
Ⓒ robin
Ⓓ owl

9. What symbols on the United States flag stand for the first 13 colonies?
Ⓐ stars
Ⓑ white stripes
Ⓒ red stripes
Ⓓ red and white stripes

10. What did the Declaration of Independence do?
Ⓐ It told England that Americans wanted their freedom.
Ⓑ It told England to send more people to live in America.
Ⓒ England told America it needed to pay more taxes.
Ⓓ England told America it did not have to follow England's laws.

GO ON ⇨

UNIT 1: HISTORY

Part 1, page 3

Directions Use the time line to answer exercises 11 through 14.

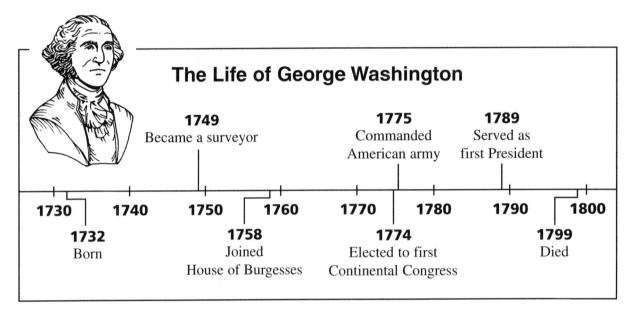

The Life of George Washington

| 1749 | 1775 | 1789 |
| Became a surveyor | Commanded American army | Served as first President |

1730   1740   1750   1760   1770   1780   1790   1800

1732 Born

1758 Joined House of Burgesses

1774 Elected to first Continental Congress

1799 Died

11. What did Washington do in 1775?
   Ⓐ farmed Mount Vernon
   Ⓑ commanded the American army
   Ⓒ served as President
   Ⓓ died

12. What year did Washington become a surveyor?
   Ⓐ 1739
   Ⓑ 1740
   Ⓒ 1749
   Ⓓ 1750

13. How old was Washington when he became a surveyor?
   Ⓐ 17
   Ⓑ 19
   Ⓒ 25
   Ⓓ 49

14. Washington was President for 8 years. What year did his presidency end?
   Ⓐ 1781
   Ⓑ 1789
   Ⓒ 1793
   Ⓓ 1797

STOP

Your time: _____   Number right: _____

Name _____   Date _____

UNIT 1: HISTORY

Part 2: Short Answer

Directions   Read the paragraph and study the diagram. Think about information you know about the Indians living on the plains. Use complete sentences to answer the questions.

You have 15 minutes.

   The Omaha Indians, like many American Indians on the Great Plains, moved around the land. They followed the herds of buffalo. The buffalo provided food, clothing, and shelter. The shelter the Indians lived in was called a *tepee*.

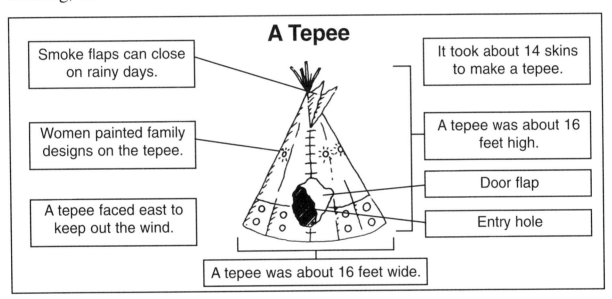

A Tepee

Smoke flaps can close on rainy days.

Women painted family designs on the tepee.

A tepee faced east to keep out the wind.

It took about 14 skins to make a tepee.

A tepee was about 16 feet high.

Door flap

Entry hole

A tepee was about 16 feet wide.

1. How many buffalo skins did it take to make a tepee?

_____

2. What was the width and height of a tepee?

_____

3. Why were tepees a good kind of shelter for the Indians living on the Great Plains?

_____

_____

GO ON ⇨

UNIT 1: HISTORY

Part 2, page 2

Directions   Study the map. Use complete sentences to answer exercises 4 through 6.

Population Map of New York

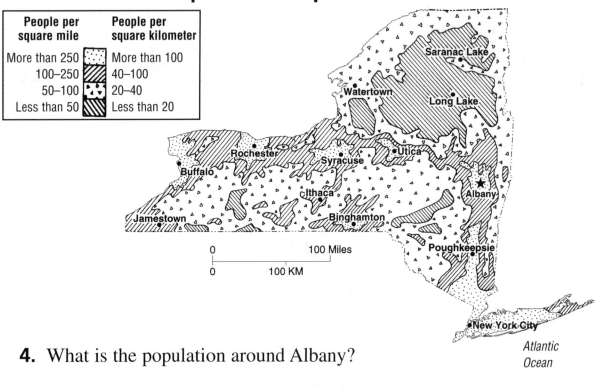

4. What is the population around Albany?

   _____

5. Are there more people living around Long Lake or Watertown? Explain.

   _____

   _____

6. New York is the largest city in the U.S. Trade is an important business in this city. How does the location help the city's business?

   _____

   _____

   _____

UNIT 1: HISTORY

Part 3: Extended Response

Directions Study the picture.
Think about other information you know
related to how people traveled long ago.
Then, complete the exercise.

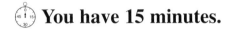 **You have 15 minutes.**

How did people travel long ago?
How do people travel now?
How are the ways of travel alike
and different?

Be sure to...

use complete sentences.

give examples.

write neatly.

_____

_____

_____

_____

_____

_____

_____

_____

_____

GO ON ⇨

UNIT 1: HISTORY

Part 3, page 2

_____

_____

_____

_____

_____

_____

_____

_____

_____

_____

Reread your answer to see that you...

    used complete sentences.

    gave examples.

    wrote neatly.

_____

Your time: _____

On this lesson I did _____ because _____

_____.

UNIT 2: GEOGRAPHY

Part 1: Multiple Choice

Directions   Darken the circle by the correct answer.

Sample:

Which of these names a model of the Earth?

Ⓐ world map
Ⓑ globe
Ⓒ compass rose
Ⓓ pictograph

Answer

The correct answer is *B*. A *globe* is a sphere that shows the shape of the Earth and its landforms.

Now Try These

⏱ **You have 15 minutes.**

1. Where could you find tall office buildings and subways?

Ⓐ in a suburb
Ⓑ in a city
Ⓒ in a town
Ⓓ on a farm

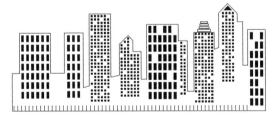

2. What is a place where ships can stay safe from high waves and strong winds?

Ⓐ coast
Ⓑ gateway
Ⓒ harbor
Ⓓ deck

3. What is something found in nature that is useful to people?

Ⓐ natural resource
Ⓑ money
Ⓒ car
Ⓓ capital city

4. What is a make-believe line around the center of the Earth?

Ⓐ equator
Ⓑ pole
Ⓒ zone
Ⓓ hemisphere

GO ON ⇨

UNIT 2: GEOGRAPHY

Part 1, page 2

5. Which of these is a physical feature?
   Ⓐ factory
   Ⓑ lake
   Ⓒ boat
   Ⓓ bridge

6. Which of these names a mineral?
   Ⓐ cattle
   Ⓑ corn
   Ⓒ fish
   Ⓓ gold

7. Which is a growing season?
   Ⓐ the water needed to make the crops grow
   Ⓑ the soils crops need
   Ⓒ the months crops can grow
   Ⓓ the resources crops make

8. What area is best for farming?
   Ⓐ city
   Ⓑ plain
   Ⓒ mountain
   Ⓓ business area

9. What is a large, raised part of land?
   Ⓐ mountain
   Ⓑ island
   Ⓒ pasture
   Ⓓ desert

10. What is the usual weather of a place?
   Ⓐ dry
   Ⓑ crop
   Ⓒ climate
   Ⓓ summer

GO ON ⇨

Name _____   Date _____

UNIT 2: GEOGRAPHY

Part 1, page 3

Directions   Use the map to answer exercises 11 through 14.

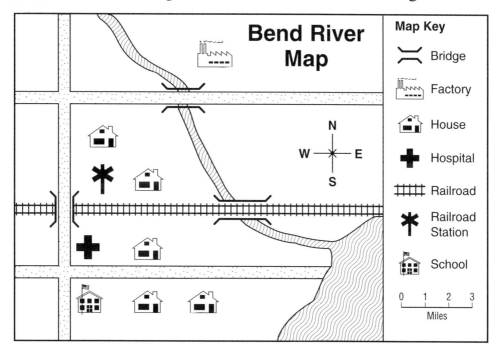

11. What does ✚ mean?
- Ⓐ church
- Ⓑ school
- Ⓒ house
- Ⓓ hospital

12. In what part of the city is the factory?
- Ⓐ north
- Ⓑ south
- Ⓒ east
- Ⓓ west

13. About how far is it from the railroad station to the school?
- Ⓐ about 1 mile
- Ⓑ about 3 miles
- Ⓒ about 5 miles
- Ⓓ about 9 miles

14. In which direction will you travel if you leave the school and drive to the lake?
- Ⓐ north
- Ⓑ south
- Ⓒ east
- Ⓓ west

STOP

Your time: _____   Number right: _____

UNIT 2: GEOGRAPHY

Part 2: Short Answer

Directions Study the landform map of the state of Washington. Use complete sentences to answer exercises 1 through 4.

🕐 **You have 25 minutes.**

Landforms in Washington

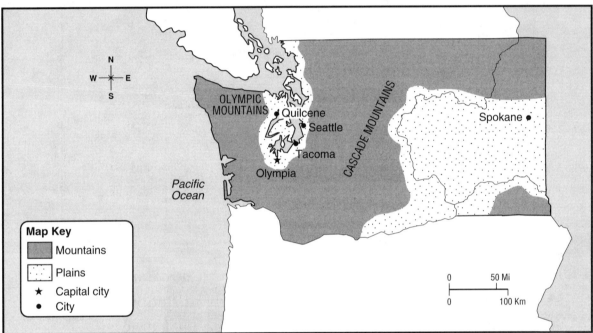

1. What is the capital of the state of Washington?

   _____

2. What kind of landform covers most of Washington?

   _____

3. What landform is found along the coast of the Pacific Ocean?

   _____

4. In what part of the state are most farms found? Explain.

   _____

   _____

GO ON ⇨

Name _____ Date _____

UNIT 2: GEOGRAPHY

Part 2, page 2

Directions Study the map. Then, use complete sentences to answer exercises 5 through 7.

Regions of the United States

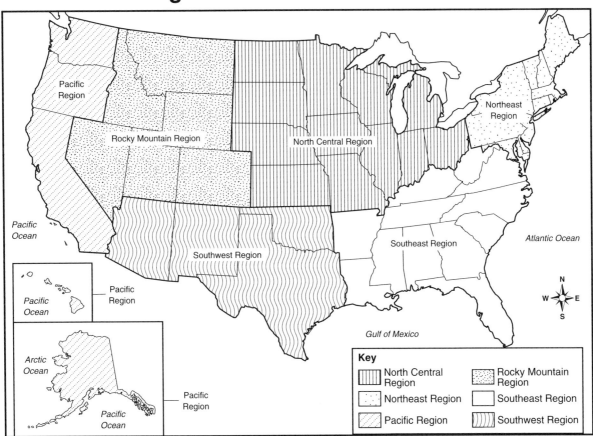

5. How many regions are in the United States?

_____

6. How did the Pacific Region most likely get its name?

_____

7. Through which two bodies of water would you travel to go by water from the Northeast Region to the Southwest Region?

_____

UNIT 2: GEOGRAPHY

Part 2, page 3

Directions   Read the paragraphs. Use complete sentences to answer the question.

Inuits, also called Eskimos, have lived in the far north for thousands of years. They hunted walruses, seals, whales, and polar bears. From these animals, the Inuits got food, skins for clothing, and oil for heating and light. They also made houses from animal skins or blocks of snow. They used dog sleds to travel.

Today, Inuits live in modern houses with electricity. Inuit children attend schools. Also, most Inuits now use snowmobiles instead of dog sleds.

How did the Inuits use their environment to meet their needs?

_____

_____

_____

_____

_____ STOP

UNIT 2: GEOGRAPHY

Part 3: Extended Response

Directions Study the map. Think about other information you know related to the five geography themes. Then, complete the exercise.

You have 15 minutes.

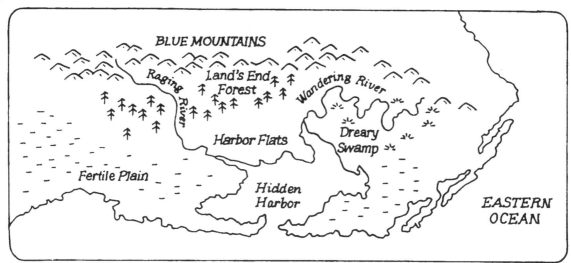

Imagine that you are part of a group of people looking for a good place to live. You want a place that will have food, water, and shelter. You are offered the area above to settle. Will it suit your needs?

Be sure to...

use complete sentences.

give examples.

write neatly.

_____

_____

_____

_____

_____

_____

GO ON ⇨

UNIT 2: GEOGRAPHY

Part 3, page 2

_____

_____

_____

_____

_____

_____

_____

_____

_____

_____

_____

Reread your answer to see that you...

    used complete sentences.

    gave examples.

    wrote neatly.

_____

Your time: _____

On this lesson I did _____ because _____

_____

_____.

UNIT 3: GOVERNMENT

Part 1: Multiple Choice

Directions Darken the circle by the correct answer.

Sample:

What are members of the Supreme Court called?

Ⓐ governors
Ⓑ branches
Ⓒ presidents
Ⓓ justices

Answer

The correct answer is *D*. The Supreme Court makes sure the laws in the country are carried out fairly. These people are called *justices*.

Now Try These

⏱ **You have 15 minutes.**

1. What are the President and Congress part of?
   Ⓐ state government
   Ⓑ national government
   Ⓒ Supreme Court
   Ⓓ community government

2. What is the name of a person who lives in a community?
   Ⓐ citizen
   Ⓑ pioneer
   Ⓒ ancestor
   Ⓓ jury

3. Which branch of the government sees that the laws are carried out fairly?
   Ⓐ judicial
   Ⓑ executive
   Ⓒ federal
   Ⓓ legislative

4. Which right in the Bill of Rights allows people to gather in a public place to show they do not like something?
   Ⓐ Freedom of the Press
   Ⓑ Freedom of Religion
   Ⓒ Freedom of Assembly
   Ⓓ Freedom to Have a Trial by Jury

GO ON ⇨

UNIT 3: GOVERNMENT

Part 1, page 2

5. Who helps the mayor make sure things get done?

  Ⓐ parent

  Ⓑ lawyer

  Ⓒ judge

  Ⓓ city manager

6. Which of these means "to choose or vote"?

  Ⓐ call

  Ⓑ elect

  Ⓒ ballot

  Ⓓ court

7. Who is the leader of a state?

  Ⓐ President

  Ⓑ mayor

  Ⓒ Congress

  Ⓓ governor

8. What is the capital of the United States?

  Ⓐ Washington, D.C.

  Ⓑ New York City, New York

  Ⓒ Richmond, Virginia

  Ⓓ Olympia, Washington

9. What is the money people pay to support the government and its services?

  Ⓐ loans

  Ⓑ interest

  Ⓒ taxes

  Ⓓ stock

10. Which of these names something a responsible citizen does?

  Ⓐ Mara picks up trash off the ground.

  Ⓑ Sam leaves his lunch bag on the cafeteria table.

  Ⓒ Pam runs in the hall at school.

  Ⓓ Eric rides his bike on a busy sidewalk.

GO ON ⇨

UNIT 3: GOVERNMENT

Part 1, page 3

Directions Study the diagram to answer exercises 11 through 14.

Uses of City Tax Money

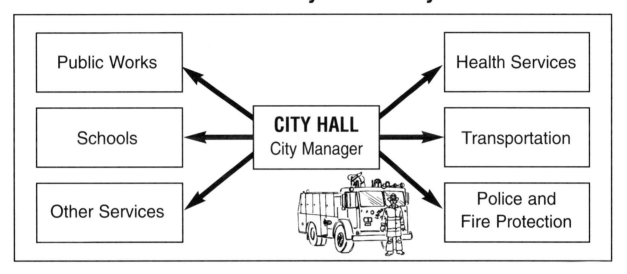

11. Who pays the people working for a city?
Ⓐ President
Ⓑ governor
Ⓒ judge
Ⓓ city manager

12. For what part of the city government does a bus driver work?
Ⓐ transportation
Ⓑ health services
Ⓒ police protection
Ⓓ public works

13. For what part of the city government do people in the water area work?
Ⓐ health services
Ⓑ public works
Ⓒ schools
Ⓓ transportation

14. Which of these is NOT a part of the schools?
Ⓐ librarian
Ⓑ teacher
Ⓒ principal
Ⓓ fire chief

STOP

Your time: _____   Number right: _____

UNIT 3: GOVERNMENT

Part 2: Short Answer

Directions   Use the bar graph to answer exercises 1 through 3.
Use complete sentences to answer the questions.

⏱ **You have 15 minutes.**

Votes for Mayor of the City of Chillout

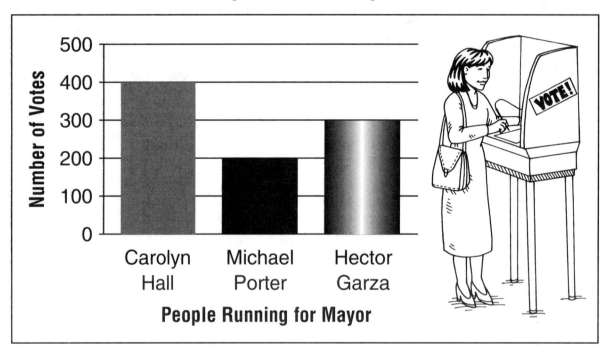

1. How many votes did Michael Porter receive?

_____

2. How many more people voted for Hector Garza than for Michael
Porter?

_____

3. Who is the new mayor of Chillout? Explain how you know.

_____

_____

GO ON ⇨

UNIT 3: GOVERNMENT

Part 2, page 2

Directions   Read the paragraph. Then, complete the exercise.

You told Justin and Maurice you would meet them by the swings at the park. When you get there, your two friends are already playing on the swings. There is one swing not in use, so you head toward it. Just as you start to sit down, you are pushed away by a girl whom you have never seen before. She grabs the swing and begins to swing on it.

The chart below shows the steps for ways to resolve a conflict. Complete the chart to show how you would follow the steps to settle the disagreement.

Ways to Resolve a Conflict

Tell the cause of the conflict.	_____ _____
Tell what each side wants.	_____ _____
Decide what each side wants most and what each side is willing to give up.	_____ _____ _____
Look for ways that each side can get most of what it wants.	_____

STOP

UNIT 3: GOVERNMENT

Part 3: Extended Response

Directions Read the paragraph. Think about other information you know related to choices people make. Then, complete the exercise.

You have 15 minutes.

Rules and laws help people make choices. They tell us what is fair and how we should act. Rules and laws are made to keep everyone safe and healthy. Each family, school, and community has rules.

What are some rules or laws that are in your family, school, and community? Give an example of each and the reason for the rule.

Be sure to...

use complete sentences.

give examples.

write neatly.

_____

_____

_____

_____

_____

_____

_____

_____

_____

GO ON ⇨

UNIT 3: GOVERNMENT

Part 3, page 2

_____

_____

_____

_____

_____

_____

_____

_____

_____

_____

_____

Reread your answer to see that you...

    used complete sentences.

    gave examples.

    wrote neatly.

STOP

Your time: _____

On this lesson I did _____ because _____

_____

_____.

Name _____ Date _____

UNIT 4: ECONOMICS

Part 1: Multiple Choice

Directions Darken the circle by the correct answer.

Sample:

Which of these is a service job?

Ⓐ making bicycles
Ⓑ fixing cars
Ⓒ growing watermelons
Ⓓ mining coal

Answer

The correct answer is *B*. A person in a service job does something directly for another person. *Fixing cars* is a job done directly for another person.

Now Try These

⏱ **You have 10 minutes.**

1. Where are computers made?
   Ⓐ in factories
   Ⓑ in offices
   Ⓒ in harbors
   Ⓓ in parks

2. What are two needs people have?
   Ⓐ toys and books
   Ⓑ clothes and cars
   Ⓒ pets and coats
   Ⓓ food and shelter

3. What is an import product?
   Ⓐ a product made for the first time
   Ⓑ a product sold to another country
   Ⓒ a product sold only in markets
   Ⓓ a product brought into a country from another country

4. What is the purpose of an advertisement?
   Ⓐ to sell products or services
   Ⓑ to entertain people
   Ⓒ to teach people what is important
   Ⓓ to make people work harder

GO ON ⇨

UNIT 4: ECONOMICS

Part 1, page 2

5. What are human resources?
- Ⓐ raw materials
- Ⓑ people who work for a company
- Ⓒ money used to buy products
- Ⓓ marketing plans

6. Which of these names when many people want the same product or service?
- Ⓐ demand
- Ⓑ supply
- Ⓒ insurance
- Ⓓ trade

7. Which of these tells about a consumer?
- Ⓐ Janie mows lawns every week to earn money.
- Ⓑ Mr. Bennett grows peaches on his farm.
- Ⓒ Jim uses birthday money to buy a circus ticket.
- Ⓓ Miss Chang rents apartments to people.

8. What is something that makes land, water, and air unclean?
- Ⓐ breeze
- Ⓑ canal
- Ⓒ spring water
- Ⓓ pollution

9. What is competition?
- Ⓐ when different companies make and sell the same product
- Ⓑ when products are sent to many different countries
- Ⓒ when people do not buy a product any more
- Ⓓ when a company makes something that another company uses

10. What is money put in a bank and kept there?
- Ⓐ loan
- Ⓑ wage
- Ⓒ savings
- Ⓓ charge

STOP

Your time: _____   Number right: _____

UNIT 4: ECONOMICS

Part 2: Short Answer

Directions Use the pictograph to answer exercises 1 through 3.

You have 15 minutes.

Josh's Market Sales for 1 Week

Type of Vegetable	Number of Vegetables Sold
Asparagus	🌱🌱🌱🌱🌱🌱🌱
Corn	🌽🌽🌽🌽🌽
Lettuce	🥬🥬🥬🥬🥬
Pumpkins	🎃🎃🎃🎃🎃🎃
Tomatoes	🍅🍅🍅🍅🍅🍅🍅🍅🍅

Key

Each symbol stands for 5 vegetables sold.

1. How many heads of lettuce were sold?

_____

2. Which vegetable did Josh sell the most of? How many did he sell?

_____

_____

3. Which two vegetables sold in equal amounts? How many of each were sold?

_____

_____ **GO ON** ⇨

UNIT 4: ECONOMICS

Part 2, page 2

Directions Use the advertisements to answer exercises 4 through 7. Use complete sentences.

September Special

CARRY-ALL BACKPACK

- Sturdy, adjustable straps
- Heavy-duty zippers
- Waterproof material
- Holds up to 40 pounds
- Colors of red, blue, and green

Only **$19.95**

Back-To-School Sale

SUNNY DAYS BACKPACK

- Popular designs
- 3 extra pockets
- Comes in 6 exciting colors

Yours for $17.95

---

4. Which backpack costs less?

_____

_____

5. Which advertisement gives more information?

_____

_____

6. Do the backpacks have the same features? Explain.

_____

_____

_____

7. How else could you compare the quality of the two backpacks before you choose one?

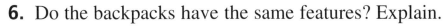

_____

_____

UNIT 4: ECONOMICS

Part 3: Extended Response

Directions   Study the map of Collinsville. Think about other information you know related to services and products. Then, complete the exercise.

🕐 **You have 15 minutes.**

Collinsville Map

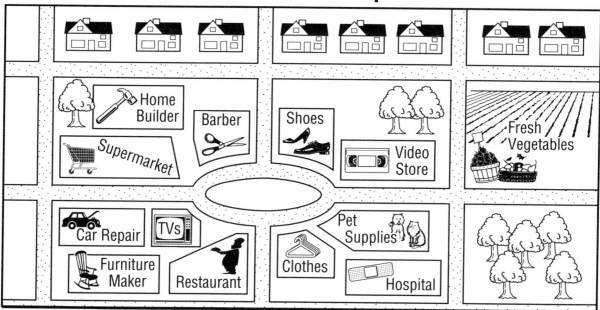

Explain the difference between producers and people who offer services. Use examples from the map in your explanation.

Be sure to...

use complete sentences.

give examples.

write neatly.

_____

_____

_____

_____

UNIT 4: ECONOMICS

Part 3, page 2

_____

_____

_____

_____

_____

_____

_____

_____

_____

_____

_____

_____

Reread your answer to see that you...

    used complete sentences.

    gave examples.

    wrote neatly.

STOP

Your time: _____

On this lesson I did _____ because _____

_____

_____.

Higher Scores on Social Studies Standardized Tests, Grade 3

Answer Key

History Pretest, Part 1, page 4
1. B   4. B
2. C   5. A
3. A   6. D

History Pretest, Part 2, page 5
7. 1800 to 1880
8. 1806
9. Omaha became the capital first.
10. 24 years

Geography Pretest, Part 1, page 6
1. D   4. B
2. C   5. A
3. A   6. B

Geography Pretest, Part 2, page 7
Answers will vary. Possible response: A community is a group of people who live together in the same place and work to make it a good place to live. Henryville is a good community because:

• the weather is mild.

• there are many places to work.

• there are many services.

• people help each other meet needs.

Government Pretest, Part 1, page 8
1. C   4. A
2. B   5. C
3. A   6. D

Government Pretest, Part 2, page 9
Answers will vary. Students should address the letter to the governor or to a state representative. Make sure students provide two details to support their opinion.

Economics Pretest, Part 1, page 10
1. A   4. C
2. D   5. A
3. D   6. B

Economics Pretest, Part 2, page 11
7. Tobacco is the product grown closest to the capital.
8. Hogs, poultry, and corn are found near Rose Hill.
9. The land is probably flat, and the soil is the right kind to grow those kind of crops.

General Posttest, Part 1, pages 12–13
1. C   6. D
2. D   7. A
3. C   8. C
4. B   9. B
5. C   10. C

General Posttest, Part 2, page 14
1. Phoenix gets 10 to 20 inches of rain each year.
2. The eastern part of Oklahoma gets 40 to 60 inches each year.
3. There is not enough rain for farming in western Texas, so crops will not grow.

General Posttest, Part 2, page 15
Possible comparisons: walls made of logs, mud used between logs, notched ends, dirt floor;

Possible contrasts: hogan shaped like a hexagon—cabin shaped like a rectangle;

hogan had smoke hole in roof center—cabin had chimney at one end;

hogan had mud roof—cabin had rough boards made from logs.

General Posttest, Part 3, pages 16–17
Answers will vary. Possible responses:

• built near water.

• built where people meet people.

• built near resources.

• built for government.

Answer Key, continued

History, Part 1, pages 18–20

1. C	**8.** B
2. B	**9.** D
3. D	**10.** A
4. A	**11.** B
5. D	**12.** C
6. A	**13.** A
7. C	**14.** D

History, Part 2, page 21

1. It took about 14 skins to make a tepee.

2. A tepee was about 16 feet high and 16 feet wide at the base.

3. Possible responses: The Indians on the Great Plains moved frequently. The tepees were light and easy to pick up and move. Also, there were few trees on the plains. The tepees were good because they were made from the buffalo skins.

History, Part 2, page 22

4. There are more than 250 people per square mile around Albany.

5. There are more people around Watertown. The key shows 50 to 100 people per square mile around Watertown. There are fewer than 50 per square mile around Long Lake.

6. The city is located near the Atlantic Ocean, so goods can easily be moved in and out of the city.

History, Part 3, pages 23–24

Answers will vary. Possible response: Long ago people used horses, wagons, and big sailing ships. Today people use cars, trains, trucks, airplanes, and ships. They are alike in the use of ships to cross water, even though old ships used wind power and modern ships use fuel. The transportation is mostly different, because we have developed different fuels and many kinds of technology.

Geography, Part 1, pages 25–27

1. B	**8.** B
2. C	**9.** A
3. A	**10.** C
4. A	**11.** D
5. B	**12.** A
6. D	**13.** C
7. C	**14.** C

Geography, Part 2, pages 28–29

1. Olympia is the capital of Washington.

2. Mountains cover most of Washington.

3. Mountains are found along the coast.

4. Most farms are probably found in the east on the plains because they are flat and have better soil.

5. The map shows six regions in the United States.

6. It got its name because the Pacific Ocean is the western border for those states.

7. To travel from the Northeast to the Southwest Region, you would cross the Atlantic Ocean and Gulf of Mexico.

Geography, Part 2, page 30

Possible responses: People have needs for food, shelter, and clothing. The Inuits hunted animals for food. Skins from the animals were used for clothing and shelter. Some parts of the animals provided oil to heat and light the shelters. The Inuits used snow for shelter, too. Finally, movement was done with sleds over the snow and ice. Dogs pulled the sleds.

Answer Key, continued

Geography, Part 3, pages 31–32

Make sure students use complete sentences and give examples. Students should note that the area would be a good place for several of the following reasons:

- a plain to grow crops for food.
- rivers provide drinking water, fishing, and other resources.
- forests to build shelter.
- mountains provide mineral resources.
- harbor provides a safe place to dock ships and to fish.
- swamp could be a drawback or a natural area for wildlife.

Government, Part 1, pages 33–35

1. B	**8.** A
2. A	**9.** C
3. A	**10.** A
4. C	**11.** D
5. D	**12.** A
6. B	**13.** B
7. D	**14.** D

Government, Part 2, page 36

1. Michael Porter received 200 votes.
2. Hector Garza received 100 more votes.
3. Carolyn Hall is the new mayor, because the bar graph shows she received more votes than the other people.

Government, Part 2, page 37

Possible responses:
Cause: Two people want the same swing.
Wants: Two people want to swing.
Wants most and most willing to give up:
Answers will vary.
Look for ways to resolve: Answers will vary.

Government, Part 3, pages 38–39

Accept reasonable answers. Make sure students cite one rule each for community, school, and family. Possible responses:

- Community: Cars and bikes must stop at stop signs to keep them from crashing and hurting people.
- School: Students can not shout in the halls since shouting will disrupt learning and studying.
- Family: I must be in bed by 8:30 so that I will be rested and stay healthy.

Economics, Part 1, pages 40–41

1. A	**6.** A
2. D	**7.** C
3. D	**8.** D
4. A	**9.** A
5. B	**10.** C

Economics, Part 2, page 42

1. 25 heads
2. tomatoes; 50
3. corn and pumpkins; 30

Economics, Part 2, page 43

4. The Sunny Days Backpack costs less.
5. The Carry-All Backpack gives more information.
6. We do not know if the Sunny Days Backpack has the same features as the Carry-All Backpack since they are not listed on the advertisement.
7. You would have to look at both backpacks to compare the features each has before choosing.

Economics, Part 3, pages 44–45

Answers will vary. Possible response: A producer is a person or company that makes or creates something. The furniture maker, home builder, and vegetable grower are all examples of people who make something. A service is a helpful act or a kind of work done for another person. A hospital, barber, car repair shop, and restaurant offer a service.